Tom McGowen

SINK THE
BISMARCK

GERMANY'S
SUPER-BATTLESHIP
OF WORLD WAR II

TWENTY-FIRST CENTURY BOOKS

Brookfield, Connecticut

Cover and book designed by Joan O'Connor.

Cover photograph courtesy of Bildarchiv Preussischer Kulturbesitz (bpk), Berlin
Photographs courtesy of AP/Wide World Photos: pp. 4, 10, 11, 20, 24; Ullstein
Bilderdienst: p. 13; UPI/Corbis-Bettmann: pp. 15, 23, 36, 54, 55, 61; © Bildarchiv
Preussischer Kulturbesitz (bpk), Berlin: p. 16; Public Record Office Image Library:
p. 18; U. S. Government Navy Naval Historical Center/NGS Image Sales: pp. 26, 27;
The Illustrated London News Picture Library: p. 44,; Hulton Getty/Liaison Agency;
p. 49; Bilderdienst Suddeutscher Verlag: p. 58

Library of Congress Cataloging in Publication Data

McGowen, Tom.
Sink the Bismarck: Germany's super battleship of World War II/
Tom McGowen.
p. cm.—(Military might)
Includes index.
Summary: Describes the actions of the German battleship "Bismarck"
during World War II and the operations of the British navy to destroy this ship.
ISBN 0-7613-1510-1 (lib. bdg.)
1. Bismarck (Battleship) Juvenile literature. [1. World War, 1939-1945—Naval
operations, German Juvenile literature. 2.Bismarck (Battleship) 3. World War,
1939–1945—Naval operations, German.] I. Title. II. Series.
D722.B5 M24 1999 940.54'5943 dc21   98-48500 CIP AC

Published by Twenty-First Century Books
A Division of The Millbrook Press, Inc.
2 Old New Milford Road
Brookfield, Connecticut 06804

Contents

Chapter 1

THE WARSHIPS OF 1941

At two o'clock in the morning darkness of May 19, in the year 1941, a huge sleek shape moved quietly out of the waters of a seaport in eastern Germany, and turned northwest. The world's most powerful warship, the German battleship *Bismarck*, was heading out to sea, to do its part in its country's war against Great Britain, the war that was to become known as World War II.

The war had begun in 1939, when the armies of Germany had invaded Poland. France and Great Britain (which then included Britain, Canada, Australia, New Zealand, India, and a number of other countries) had immediately declared war on Germany.

Great Britain had a rather small army of about only 400,000 men, most of which it sent to France to help in the fighting that would take place against Germany. But its navy was the largest and most powerful in the world, with far more ships than the

The German battleship Bismarck *was the most powerful warship in the world in 1941.*

German Navy. In battleships alone, Great Britain had eighteen to Germany's four, and in the kind of ships called cruisers it had seventy-seven to thirteen! It would have been suicide for the German Navy to try to fight the British on equal terms, so the German naval commanders decided that the best use for their ships would be to strike at Great Britain's merchant shipping, the ships that brought goods and materials to Britain from other countries. The island of Britain, containing the united countries of England, Scotland, and Wales, was the heart of Great Britain, and depended almost entirely upon such shipping for its survival—shipments of beef, butter, wheat, fuel oil, rubber, copper, machinery, and other essential supplies, brought from Canada, the United States, and other countries. If large amounts of those supplies could be destroyed before they reached Britain, Britain's ability to manufacture weapons and feed its armies, as well as its civilian population, would be seriously affected. And so, German submarines and surface warships began to slip out into the Atlantic Ocean to prey upon the merchant ships making their way toward Britain.

The German Army, well trained and well equipped, con-quered Poland in less than a month. In the early spring of 1940, Germany invaded and quickly conquered Denmark and Norway, to use them as air and naval bases against Britain. Then, in May, Germany launched a whirlwind invasion of Belgium, the Netherlands, and France. In only forty-seven days all three nations were crushed and conquered by the "lightning war" tactics of the swift-moving German tank divisions, operat-ing with the help of the German Air Force's deadly *Stuka* dive-bombers. The shattered remnants of the small British Army that had been sent to help France were evacuated from France by sea in a daring rescue operation involving hundreds of British ships of all kinds.

Britain now stood alone against Germany. For a time, the people of Britain expected to be invaded by German forces at any moment. Actually, Adolf Hitler, the man who was absolute ruler of Germany, *was* planning an invasion. Throughout the months of August and September, the German Air Force made thousands of air attacks on Britain—bombing airfields, factories, and cities—in an attempt to "soften up" the country for invasion. But the bombing raids were fairly unsuccessful, and Hitler finally called the invasion off.

Hitler and his advisers had decided that instead of trying to conquer Britain they could simply wear it down by applying pressure in a number of different ways. For one, the German Navy was urged to step up its campaign against British shipping, which was working very well. More than two and a half million tons of shipments had been destroyed since the beginning of the war, and even a number of British warships, including the giant battleship *Royal Oak*, had been sunk by German submarines and warships. As a result, Britain was experiencing food shortages, fuel rationing, and other problems. The German leaders felt that if the people of Britain got sufficiently hungry, cold, and dispirited, they might become willing to surrender if Germany offered reasonable terms that were not harsh. And so a deadly struggle began between the navies of Great Britain and Germany. For Germany, it was an effort to reduce the amount of supplies getting to Britain to the tiniest trickle. For the British, it was the need to protect its shipping by literally destroying most of Germany's navy, if possible.

The ships and weapons of the navies involved in this struggle were not much like the ships and weapons of today. There were no guided missiles; ships had only large cannons that fired explosive projectiles and torpedoes that simply went wherever they were aimed. There were no helicopters, no jet airplanes. No ships had nuclear-powered engines. Ships burned oil for fuel, and their captains had to base all plans around being able to get more oil when they needed it. Computers as we know them did not yet exist, and radar was fairly primitive. Messages from ships, airplanes, and bases were sent by means of radio, using the dots and dashes of Morse code.

Today, aircraft carriers are generally regarded as the most important ships in a navy, but in the early days of World War II the majority of naval officers felt that the most important kind of ship was the battleship. These were the most powerful of warships. The size of a warship's guns is generally indicated by the *width* of the projectiles they fire, and the main guns of battleships were among the biggest of all guns, firing explosive projectiles called shells that were 12, 14, or 16 inches wide, several feet long, and as much as two tons in weight. Basically, a battleship was simply a huge floating platform for a number of such giant guns, which could send shells screaming through the air for distances of 15 miles or more. This meant that a battleship could stay out of the range of smaller guns on smaller ships, and smash those ships to pieces with its big weapons. On the other hand, battleships were so heavily armored with thick sheets of steel mixed with other strong metals, that they could often withstand the explosions of shells that hit them without taking much damage. Thus, a battleship was equal to a number of smaller warships, and was overwhelmingly superior to unarmed merchant ships, so that even a single battleship was a terrible threat to enemy shipping in time of war. An average battleship was from 700 to 800 feet long, with eight to ten big guns, and a crew of about 1,500 to 2,000 men (there were no women on any navy ships in those days).

The next most important ship in a navy was the cruiser. A cruiser was smaller than a battleship and had smaller guns, the biggest generally being about 8 inches in size, but it was fairly heavily armored and could take a lot of punishment. It was faster than a battleship and could go farther before needing to refuel. There were two kinds of cruisers, known as light cruisers and heavy cruisers, depending on whether the size of their guns was 6 or 8 inches. Cruisers sometimes had torpedo tubes, for launching torpedoes into the water, and often had one or more airplanes, that could be literally "shot" into the air by means of a catapult—actually, a kind of slingshot! These were "seaplanes," with floats instead of wheels, so they could come down in the water and be picked up by the ship, with a crane. Such planes were mostly used for scouting. A single cruiser was no match for a battleship, but two or more of them might give a battleship a good fight. A cruiser was generally about 600 feet long, with a crew of about 850 men.

The ships called destroyers were smaller and faster than a cruiser, able to make quick turns. Their main job was to protect bigger, slower ships, such as battleships and transports, which carried troops, from the attacks of submarines. When a submarine was seen, or heard by means of listening devices that could pick up the sound of its engines, destroyers rushed to where it was thought to be and dropped depth charges. These were containers about the size of oil drums, filled with explosives, that sank down into the water and blew up. Such an explosion close to a submarine could break open the sub's hull. Destroyers also had tubes for launching torpedoes, as well as a number of small guns, and several destroyers might be capable of ganging up on a larger ship and seriously damaging it. But destroyers had no armor and could be easily damaged themselves. An average destroyer was about 370 feet long or more, and had a crew of several hundred men.

Some of the biggest navies had a few aircraft carriers. Like the aircraft carriers of today, these were basically just floating airfields, with huge flat decks that planes could take off from and land on. Their basic purpose at the beginning of World War II was to provide a fleet of battleships, cruisers, and destroyers with a fairly large number of airplanes that could make bombing attacks on enemy ships, damaging them enough so that the battleships and other warships could finish them off.

All these were the kinds of ships with which British and

Following the launching of the Bismarck *at Hamburg, Adolf Hitler congratulated some of the workers who built the super-battleship.*

German naval commanders carried out their plans and fought their battles. They knew what each kind of ship could do and what it couldn't do. They knew that sometimes, because of new ideas and new improvements in technology, a warship would be built that was superior to anything of its kind, and they would then have to figure out ways of dealing with it, with the ships they had.

Such a ship, superior to anything of its kind, was the German battleship *Bismarck*. Construction of the *Bismarck* had begun in July 1936, and its designers had done everything they could think of to make it as fast, well protected, and *deadly* as

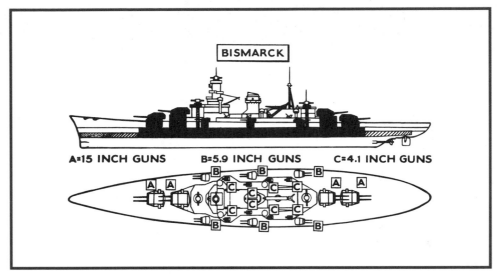

These drawings of the Bismarck *show the area of maximum armor covering her main gun turrets and magazines (in black, top). The lower illustration shows the placement of the* Bismarck's *various guns.*

possible. When it was completed in August 1940, it was regarded as the most powerful warship in the world. It had eight 15-inch guns mounted on four turrets, and twenty-eight smaller guns of 5.9- and 4.1-inch diameter. Its main gun turrets were covered with armor as much as 14 inches thick, and the armor on its sides was as much as 12 3/4 inches thick. It carried six small airplanes that could be launched from a catapult to fly ahead of the ship and scout for enemies or prey. The *Bismarck* was about 820 feet long, could move at a speed of 34 1/2 miles an hour, and could travel more than 11,000 miles before needing to refuel. It carried a crew of 2,092 men.

So, as Britain, fighting for its life, tried to prevent the German Navy from destroying its vital shipping, the British naval commanders knew that sooner or later their ships would have to face this powerful new foe. That time finally came on the nineteenth of May, 1941, when the *Bismarck* set out to do its part in the effort to bring Britain to its knees.

Chapter 2

PROBLEMS FOR THE ROYAL NAVY

The *Bismarck* was accompanied by another new ship, the *Prinz Eugen*, a 677-foot long heavy cruiser, with eight 8-inch guns and a top speed of about 38 miles an hour. The two ships were under the orders of Admiral Günther Lütjens, who made the *Bismarck* his flagship, the ship from which he commanded. The *Bismarck*'s commander was *Kapitän zur See* (sea captain) Ernst Lindemann, and the commander of the *Prinz Eugen* was *Kapitän zur See* Helmuth Brinkmann.

It was Admiral Lütjens's intention to take the ships through the area of water between Denmark and Sweden, then up along the coast of Norway, and finally to turn southwest and move through the waters between Iceland and Greenland, known as the Denmark Strait, into the Atlantic Ocean. In the Atlantic the two ships would prey upon convoys (groups of merchant ships protected by a few warships) coming from Canada to Britain. Until they turned westward, the *Bismarck* and the *Prinz Eugen* would be escorted by several destroyers, to protect them from possible submarine attacks.

The commanders of the German Navy were hoping that

Admiral Günther Lütjens had both the Bismarck *and the* Prinz Eugen
under his command.

the movement of the two ships could be kept secret from the British Navy as long as possible. But on May 20, as the *Bismarck* and the *Prinz Eugen*, escorted by their destroyers, passed between Denmark and Sweden, a Swedish warship came into sight. Sweden was a neutral country—not aligned with either Germany or the Allies—so the ship was no threat, but it immediately radioed a report on the German ships to the nearest Swedish naval base. That evening, a British naval officer attached to the British Embassy in Sweden was informed by a Swedish naval officer about the German ships and at once sent a radio message to Britain. Within minutes the commanders of the British Navy knew that two battleship-size German ships and three destroyers were moving northward from Denmark and Sweden toward Norway.

Next day, as the German warships were moving past the Norwegian coast, they were reported again. Norway had been conquered by the Germans and was occupied by German troops, but there was a vigorous underground (freedom fighter) movement in Norway, doing everything possible to cause the Germans trouble. From a hiding place on the coast several members of the underground watched the ships through binoculars, then sent a coded radio message to Britain.

Shortly, messages were being sent from British naval headquarters to the British Royal Air Force, urging that planes flying over the area where the ships had been seen try to locate them. At 1:15 on the afternoon of the next day, May 21, the pilot of a British Spitfire (fighter plane) spotted the ships lying at anchor in a harbor on the coast of Norway and photographed them. The sight of this plane flying overhead caused the *Bismarck*'s antiaircraft units to sound an alarm, but they did not fire on the plane and it sped away. A few hours later, the commanders of the British Navy were looking at the pictures.

The British commanders had been expecting an attempted "breakout" of German ships and this appeared to be it. They

British pilots and a squadron of Spitfires stand ready, somewhere in England. Photographs taken by a Spitfire pilot confirmed that German battleships were making a break for the Atlantic.

were gravely concerned. It seemed sure that the largest ship in the pictures must be the *Bismarck.* They knew a lot about the *Bismarck* as the result of the work of spies, and knew that if this powerful battleship got loose in the Atlantic the danger to British shipping would be catastrophic. Obviously, the *Bismarck* and its companion, which they now knew to be the *Prinz Eugen,* could not be allowed to get into the Atlantic. British warships would have to find them, fight them, and destroy them!

But there were a number of problems. The *Bismarck* and the *Prinz Eugen* together represented a lot of power, and it would take a sizeable force of British ships to deal with them. However, the ships that could make up such a force were badly scattered. The battleships *King George V* and *Prince of Wales,* and

The Prinz Eugen *fires one of her 8-inch guns.*

the powerful battle cruiser *Hood,* were all at the Scapa Flow naval base north of Scotland. The battleship *Repulse* and the aircraft carrier *Victorious* were getting ready to sail from southern England with a troop convoy (a number of ships carrying soldiers to the Middle East). The battleship *Renown,* the aircraft carrier *Ark Royal,* and the cruiser *Sheffield* were hundreds of miles away in the Mediterranean Sea. The cruiser *Suffolk* was patrolling the ice-filled waters between Iceland and Greenland,

and the cruiser *Norfolk* was lying at harbor in Iceland. The battleship *Rodney* was in the Atlantic, guarding a convoy.

The British commanders acted quickly, taking some dangerous chances. They ordered the battleship *Repulse* and the carrier *Victorious* to stay near England, letting the troop convoy sail without them, which meant that it had very little protection! They ordered the *Renown*, the *Ark Royal*, and the *Sheffield* to sail home at once, which left British strength in the Mediterranean Sea dangerously low.

The task of finding and fighting the two German ships belonged to Admiral Sir John Tovey, commander in chief of the British Home Fleet, which had the job of protecting Britain and British shipping. Tovey's main problem was that if the *Bismarck* and the *Prinz Eugen* tried to get into the Atlantic there were two possible routes they might take—southward, between Britain and Iceland, or northward, through the Denmark Strait between Iceland and Greenland. Therefore, the British warships would either have to be used to block one of the routes with a large force, or would have to be divided up to cover both routes with smaller forces. Tovey's first action was to send word to the cruiser *Suffolk*, patrolling the Denmark Strait, to keep a sharp lookout, and he ordered the cruiser *Norfolk*, at harbor in Iceland, to go at once to the *Suffolk*'s assistance. Then he carefully thought things over.

Tovey finally decided to send the battleship *Prince of Wales*, the battle cruiser *Hood*, and six destroyers, all under the command of Vice Admiral Lancelot Holland, to spread out and watch the Denmark Strait. Tovey himself took command of a little fleet consisting of the battleships *King George V* and *Repulse* and the carrier *Victorious*, holding them back until he could determine for sure where the *Bismarck* and the *Prinz Eugen* were going. If the German vessels took the northern route, Tovey could quickly move to join Holland's force in the Denmark Strait, forming an extremely powerful fleet. And if the Germans

In an undated photograph, Admiral Sir John Tovey (right) poses with British Prime Minister Winston Churchill (center) and Sir Stafford Cripps, a member of Churchill's Cabinet.

moved southward, Tovey could move to intercept them and engage them in battle until Holland could join him.

Meanwhile, the German ships had weighed anchor and sailed north along the Norwegian coast. At four o'clock on the morning of May 22, the three destroyers turned back and the *Bismarck* and the *Prinz Eugen* proceeded on alone. Admiral Lütjens had been notified from Germany that his ships had been detected by the British, but he was not aware that British ships were now taking to the sea to search for him, and he had the impression that most of the British fleet was in the harbor at the Scapa Flow naval base. And so, early on the rainy, foggy morning of May 23, he ordered the *Bismarck* and the *Prinz Eugen* to turn in a westerly direction and head into the Denmark Strait.

By noon the weather had cleared, and the crews of the two ships could see the bluish-green glaciers of the coast of Greenland in the distance. Actually, the clear weather was far from welcome, because it meant that any British aircraft flying in the area would easily be able to spot the ships.

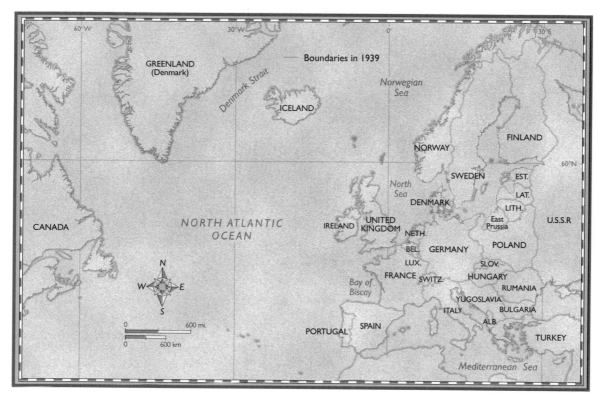

Europe and the North Atlantic

The Denmark Strait is at the edge of the Arctic Circle, and a little before seven o'clock that night the two ships moved into the pack-ice region—floating icebergs, some of enormous size and with dangerously sharp edges. It was just such a huge sharp iceberg that had caused the sinking of the *Titanic,* and the *Bismarck* and the *Prinz Eugen* had to steer careful zigzag courses in the semidarkness.

Suddenly, at 7:22, alarm bells shrilled on the *Bismarck!* The ship's radar had picked up a quick flash of another ship off in the distance. The fuzzy blip (spot of light) on the radar screen could readily be identified as a cruiser. It could only be an enemy ship.

It was, indeed, a British cruiser, the *Suffolk.* It had sighted the two German vessels and now instantly sent a radio message

The British cruiser Suffolk *was the first to spot the German ships in the Denmark Strait.*

to British Home Fleet headquarters: "One battleship, one cruiser, in sight at twenty degrees, distance seven miles, course 240 degrees."

On board the *Bismarck*, Admiral Lütjens ordered a radio message sent to German naval headquarters, reporting that his ship had sighted an enemy cruiser. On the *Suffolk*, Rear Admiral Wake-Walker, commanding both the *Suffolk* and the *Norfolk*, ordered the *Norfolk* to quickly close up with his ship.

At just about eight-thirty, alarm bells rang again on both the *Bismarck* and the *Prinz Eugen*. The *Norfolk* had been picked up on radar, and both British ships were now in gun range. There was a rush of activity as crewmen on the two German ships hurried to their battle stations. On the *Bismarck*, Captain Lindemann's voice boomed out over the intercom system. "Enemy sighted to port, our ship will accept battle!" He gave the order to commence firing.

With a thunderous crack and a flash that lit up the half-light of the arctic sky, the *Bismarck*'s guns sent a cluster of shells screaming toward the *Suffolk*. The Battle of Denmark Strait, which would last for the next four days, had begun.

Chapter 3

THE *BISMARCK* DRAWS FIRST BLOOD

The *Bismarck*'s shells fell all around the *Suffolk*, sending up tall splashes of water and throwing metal fragments onto the deck, but causing no damage. Admiral Wake-Walker knew the *Suffolk* could never risk a head-to-head fight with the German battleship, for the *Bismarck*'s guns could smash her into scrap metal. Wake-Walker ordered the *Suffolk* to lay down a smokescreen—clouds of thick smoke from the ship's smokestacks that rapidly settled down onto the surface of the water, hiding the cruiser from view. Under cover of the smoke, the *Suffolk* quickly moved out of range of the *Bismarck*'s guns, and also, of course, out of the range of the *Prinz Eugen*'s smaller guns. The *Norfolk* pulled out of range as well. One on each side, the British vessels continued to keep pace with the German ships.

Admiral Lütjens had two choices; either to try to close with the British ships and sink them, or to try to shake them off. He chose the latter. At top speed, the *Bismarck* and the *Prinz Eugen* swept through the ice floes, seeking every patch of fog and every rainsquall or snow squall, and laying brief smoke screens, in an attempt to lose the British ships. It was no use, however, for the *Suffolk* had an excellent modern radar system, far better than German radar, and was able to keep track of every move of the two German ships. At times, Lütjens tried to turn on one of the pursuers and engage it in combat, but they were always able to slip away.

In the *Bismarck*'s radio room, all of the *Suffolk*'s messages to the Home Fleet commander, Admiral Tovey, were being picked up and copied down, and Admiral Lütjens was aware that other British ships must be hurrying to join the two cruisers and do battle with his ships. He had no idea just how many were on the way, of course, but he still hoped to slip away before any arrived. At about midnight the two German ships sailed into a blinding snowstorm, and before long the radio messages from the *Suffolk* stopped. Have we gotten away from them, wondered the German crewmen.

It was not to be so. The early morning of May 24 brought beautiful clear weather, and at about 5:45, lookouts reported two ships approaching at a distance. The general quarters' alarm was sounded on both the *Bismarck* and the *Prinz Eugen*, and once again men rushed to take up their battle stations.

The two approaching ships were part of Vice Admiral Holland's force, and they were the battleship *Prince of Wales* and the battle cruiser *Hood*. The *Prince of Wales*, like the *Bismarck*, was a new ship that had been put into service less than two months earlier. It was 745 feet long, with ten 14-inch guns and sixteen 5 1/4-inch guns, and three catapult-launched airplanes. It was slightly less well armored than the *Bismarck*, and just a trifle slower.

The *Hood* was the pride of the British Navy. It was called a battle cruiser because it had been designed to have the gun power of a battleship with the speed of a cruiser. It was 860 1/2 feet long, with eight 15-inch guns, twelve 5 1/2-inch guns, and four 4-inch guns. It was fairly lightly armored—its heaviest armor, on the hull, was just 12 inches thick, as compared to the

The Prince of Wales, *along with the* Hood, *raced from Scapa Flow Naval Base north of Scotland to the Denmark Strait in pursuit of the* Bismarck.

14-inch armor on the *Bismarck*'s gun turrets—but it was just as fast as the *Bismarck*. However, the *Hood* had been put into service just after World War I, so it was now twenty-one years old. Some changes had been made on it during those years, to modernize it, but by the time World War II began, it was really a bit old-fashioned. Nevertheless, it was a deadly opponent.

Guided by the *Suffolk*'s steady reports on the position of the two German ships, the *Hood* and the *Prince of Wales* had been hurrying at full speed all through the night. The two British ships had come for the sole purpose of fighting and sinking the German vessels, and when the *Bismarck* and the *Prinz Eugen* were sighted Admiral Holland, on the *Hood*, ordered them straight ahead at the Germans.

But this actually put the two ships at a disadvantage. A warship's rotating gun turrets could be turned to either side, so that a ship with one side facing toward the enemy could fire all

The battlecruiser Hood, *a veteran of more than 20 years service, was the pride of the British Navy as battle with the* Bismarck *loomed.*

its guns, as the *Bismarck* and the *Prinz Eugen* could do. But a ship heading straight toward the enemy, as the British were doing, could only fire the guns of its front turret, straight ahead. The guns of the rear turret could not be turned to fire forward, as they were blocked by the high structure in the middle of the ship. The British also had another disadvantage; one of the *Prince of Wales*'s six forward guns was not working. Thus, the

British would begin the battle with only nine guns able to fire, while the Germans would be able to put sixteen into action.

To make things even worse for the British, Admiral Holland made two serious mistakes in his orders to his two ships. Instead of keeping a sizeable distance between the *Hood* and the *Prince of Wales,* so that the Germans would have to divide their fire between them, Holland ordered the two ships to advance close together, which actually gave the Germans a better target. Holland's other mistake was that he thought the nearest of the two German ships was the *Bismarck,* and he ordered his ships to concentrate their fire on it. But it was actually the *Prinz Eugen,* and by firing on it instead of the *Bismarck,* the British lost the chance of possibly destroying some of the *Bismarck*'s big guns before they could be used.

Moving at nearly top speed, the *Hood,* leading the two British ships, opened fire with its forward guns at a range of about 3 3/4 miles. The shells struck the water and sent up towering splashes, but the *Hood*'s target, the *Prinz Eugen,* was not hit. Aboard the *Bismarck,* gunners awaited the order to fire at the foremost of the oncoming ships, but the order did not come at once. "Request permission to fire," said the first gunnery officer over his telephone, which was connected to the ship's bridge (command area) where Admiral Lütjens and Captain Lindemann were stationed. The British ships were now beginning to turn so as to bring all their guns into action, and the Germans, seeing the extremely long shape of the front vessel immediately recognized what their opponent was. "It is the *Hood*!" exclaimed the second gunnery officer.

"Permission to fire," came the order from Captain Lindemann.

All eight of the *Bismarck*'s 20-foot-long big guns erupted with a thunderous smash that was heard all the way to the coast of Iceland, many miles away. The first salvo, or group of shells,

This photograph, taken from aboard the Prinz Eugen, *shows the* Bismarck *engulfed in a flash from its own guns, answering fire from the* Hood *and the* Prince of Wales.

fell short. The second salvo, which followed immediately, passed over the target. But seconds later, one of the shells of the third salvo exploded on the *Hood*'s deck. The battle cruiser shuddered from the impact, and a fire blazed up in one of the 4-inch gun positions. It quickly spread over the middle of the ship, and shells in a pile of ammunition began to explode like giant firecrackers.

"The enemy is burning," reported the *Bismarck*'s first gunnery officer in an exulting voice. The *Prinz Eugen* had also been firing at the *Hood*, but now Admiral Lütjens ordered it to switch its fire to the British battleship while the *Bismarck* continued to concentrate on the *Hood*. The other two British ships, the cruisers *Suffolk* and *Norfolk*, had now come into the area and began to fire, but they were still too far away and the shells from their smaller guns fell short.

The *Prince of Wales* was also now firing on the *Bismarck*, and

Following a hit from the Prince of Wales, *the* Bismarck *began flooding at her bow (front).*

the German ship was hit by a shell that passed through the hull but did no serious damage other than to make a hole that let water begin coming in. The *Bismarck* ignored the battleship and kept firing at the *Hood*. One of the shells of the *Bismarck*'s fifth salvo tore through the thin armor of the battle cruiser's main deck. It plunged straight down and exploded in the heart of the ship in the exact area where the bags of gunpowder used for firing the projectiles of the 4-inch guns were stored. Instantly, 100 tons of gunpowder blew up!

There was an eye-searing flash and a thunderous roar as a mountain-size yellowish-white fireball exploded out of the *Hood* and coiled up into the sky, slowly turning into a monstrous ball of rosy smoke. The explosion had broken the *Hood* in two and sent huge chunks of twisted metal from its hull, decks, and gun turrets whirling into the air. They came raining back down together with what looked like thousands of bright white stars, but were actually bits of molten metal that fell hissing into the sea. What had been the front part of the ship sank slowly beneath the water; the rear part drifted a short distance, then also vanished. The *Hood* was gone. Nothing was left of it but chunks and bits of floating wreckage, one large fragment of which was burning furiously and sending up a writhing plume of smoke.

The battle cruiser *Hood* had carried a crew of 1,419 men plus Admiral Holland and his staff. All but three men perished in the explosion. The three survivors were later found floating in the water by a British destroyer.

Chapter 4

A CHANGE OF PLANS

When the crew of the *Bismarck* realized that the *Hood* had been sunk, the men erupted into a frenzy of shouts, cheers, back-slapping, and hugs. Their ship had won an overwhelming victory against a very dangerous and respected enemy, and the German sailors were bursting with pride.

Aboard the *Prince of Wales* the situation was very different. The officers and men who saw the *Hood*'s destruction were shocked, stunned, and horrified. Just before the *Hood* had blown up, Admiral Holland had given the *Prince of Wales* an order to move up closer to his ship, so the battleship was now heading straight into the mass of wreckage left in the water by the explosion. It had to quickly alter course to avoid running into chunks of the *Hood*'s remains.

But the *Prince of Wales* was now at just about the same gun range from the *Bismarck* that the *Hood* had been, which gave the German ship the opportunity to fire at it without having to take the time to change the range. The command to open fire on the *Prince of Wales* was quickly given, and the *Bismarck*'s big guns thundered forth a salvo once again. Now, the sixteen main guns of both the *Prinz Eugen* and the *Bismarck* were concentrating on the British battleship.

The *Prince of Wales* began to take heavy damage. It was hit by three shells from the *Prinz Eugen*, two of them ripping through the hull below the waterline and the third bursting in a gun-loading compartment. A shell from the *Bismarck* struck the battleship's bridge, tearing straight through it without exploding, but killing everyone there except the ship's commander, Captain Leach, and one petty officer. Another *Bismarck* shell put a gun turret's fire control section (compartment where machinery for estimating ranges and loading guns was located) out of action. A third struck the crane that lifted airplanes onto the catapult and demolished it.

The *Prince of Wales* was still firing, although two of its main guns were damaged and out of action, but Captain Leach decided he had better break off combat before his ship was wrecked by the combined fire of the two German ships. He ordered a smoke screen, and cloaked by the spreading black cloud, the *Prince of Wales* turned away and retreated.

On the *Bismarck*, Admiral Lütjens and the *Bismarck*'s commander, Captain Lindemann, held a quick discussion over what to do next. Lindemann wanted to pursue the *Prince of Wales* and try to finish it off, arguing that it was badly damaged and would be easy prey. But the admiral decided against this. He apparently felt that pursuit of the British battleship might take the *Bismarck* and the *Prinz Eugen* in a direction that could bring them into contact with other British warships that were probably hurrying toward the area of the battle. This could ruin the whole plan of getting the two German ships into the Atlantic to raid British shipping. So, to the disappointment of most of the *Bismarck*'s crew, who wanted to go after the *Prince of Wales*, Lütjens elected to continue to sail in a southwesterly direction, toward the Atlantic.

With Admiral Holland dead, the commander of the three British ships was now Rear Admiral Wake-Walker, on the cruiser *Suffolk*. He, too, had a decision to make—whether to continue to force battle on the German ships or simply to go on "shadowing" them as the *Suffolk* and the *Norfolk* had been doing, keeping track of their movements until some other British ships arrived. If it came to a battle, even though the *Prince of Wales* was damaged it could still fight, and the two cruisers could lend some weight, so with luck the British might be able to inflict some serious damage on the German ships. On the other hand, the *Bismarck* and the *Prinz Eugen* together were more than a match for the three British ships, and if the battleship and two cruisers were all sunk or crippled, the Germans would be completely free to escape into the vast ocean and begin the raiding that could be a death blow to Britain. Wake-Walker decided to avoid battle and just keep following the German vessels.

However, the *Bismarck* was not destined to continue its run for the Atlantic. It had taken three hits, and when an examination of the damage was made, Lütjens realized that he would have to change his plans. Two of the hits had left holes in the *Bismarck*'s hull and water was seeping into the ship, to the extent that the additional weight of the water was causing the ship to move more slowly. Its top speed was now only a little more than 32 miles an hour. The other hit had damaged several of the fuel tanks, and the ship was leaving a broad trail of oil in the water behind it, a trail that British ships or airplanes could easily find and follow. Obviously, the *Bismarck* could not head into the Atlantic in this condition.

Once again Lütjens had to consider his options. He could try to have the damage repaired at sea while the ship was under sail, but that would require slowing down, which might give other British ships a chance to join the three now trailing the *Bismarck* and the *Prinz Eugen*. He could order the two ships to turn around and head back to Norway, which would mean the end of the whole operation. Or he could make for one of the French ports that were in German hands, have the necessary repairs made to the *Bismarck*, and then try for another break-out.

By eight o'clock in the morning, Lütjens had made up his mind. He had already sent messages to Germany informing naval headquarters of the battle and telling of the damage the *Bismarck* had suffered, and now he sent one that said: "Intention to proceed to St. Nazaire. *Prinz Eugen* cruiser warfare." What this meant was that he was going to take the *Bismarck* to the German-held French port of St. Nazaire, while the *Prinz Eugen* went on by itself to try to get out into the Atlantic and begin raiding British shipping.

But of course Lütjens could not make any moves in broad daylight in the open sea with three British ships shadowing his force every moment. He decided that the *Bismarck* and the *Prinz Eugen* should simply continue on toward the Atlantic until nightfall, then the *Bismarck* would make a big curving turn to try to draw the British off while the *Prinz Eugen* slipped away under cover of darkness. The code name selected for this maneuver was "*Hood*," and when Lütjens spoke that word over the radio, both ships were to act at once.

And so the two German warships proceeded in the direction in which they had been heading before the battle. The three British ships moved alongside them, some 18 miles away.

At about five o'clock in the afternoon the German and British ships ran into rainsqualls and a bank of fog. Visibility shrank to no more than a few miles. Immediately, Admiral Lütjens gave the order over the radio for the *Bismarck* to begin its turn and the *Prinz Eugen* to attempt to steal away—the two words: "Execute Hood!" In an effort to drive the British ships farther off, so that their radar would not be as effective, the *Bismarck* opened fire in the direction of the *Suffolk*. Officers and men on the *Prinz Eugen* watched the *Bismarck* fade out of sight in the fog, the bursts of its gunfire making red flashes in the rainy sky and on the surface of the sea.

As the *Bismarck* turned, it came back out of the fog into clearer skies, and it and the British ships became visible to one another again. The *Suffolk* quickly laid down a smoke screen and moved out of range of the *Bismarck*'s guns, but the *Prince of Wales*, at a range of 17 1/2 miles, fired a salvo at the German ship. For a time, the two ships exchanged gunfire with each other, but visibility was still poor and neither ship was hit.

Meanwhile, the *Prinz Eugen* had gotten away, as planned. On its own now, with the British ships still clinging to it, the *Bismarck* set a straight course for St. Nazaire.

Chapter 5

AN AIR ATTACK AND AN ESCAPE

The people of Britain were shocked and grieved by the news of the destruction of their prize warship, the *Hood.* The British prime minister, Winston Churchill, was awakened at seven o'clock on the morning of the twenty-fourth and given the news, which he said was a "bitter grief." He felt certain, however, that the *Bismarck* would soon be destroyed by the other British ships fighting it, and the *Hood* would be avenged. He was sharply disappointed when, an hour and a half later, he was told that the *Prince of Wales* had been forced to withdraw from combat with the *Bismarck,* and the German ship was still in good fighting shape and heading in a new direction.

The *Bismarck*'s sudden turn toward the south had completely disrupted British plans. When the Home Fleet commander, Admiral Tovey, had learned that the *Bismarck* and the *Prinz Eugen* were moving into the Denmark Strait he had moved his entire force of two battleships, an aircraft carrier, and a number of cruisers and destroyers toward the strait. He was confident that if the two German ships managed to break through the *Hood* and the *Prince of Wales,* he would be able to intercept them and sink them before they could get into the Atlantic. But now,

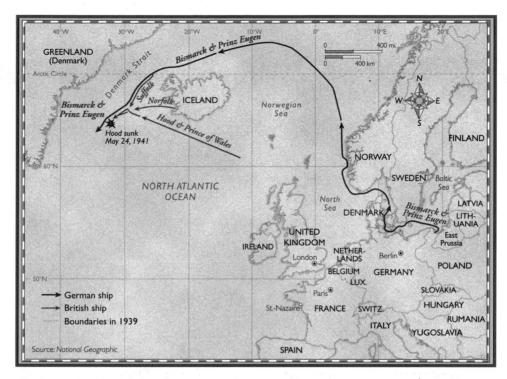

Sinking the Hood

the *Prinz Eugen* had vanished and the *Bismarck* was heading in a different direction. At the moment it was more than 630 miles away from Tovey's ships, and he had almost no hope of being able to catch up to it.

Tovey now had to try to figure out what the *Bismarck* was up to. Was it going home to Germany, was it heading for a French port, or was it going to turn west around the tip of Greenland and head back toward the Atlantic? Tovey decided that the last possibility was the most likely one, so he ordered his force to head for Greenland. Meanwhile, there was one other thing he could do. The aircraft carrier *Victorious* was a new ship that had been sent out in the emergency without its full amount of aircraft; it had only one flight of nine Swordfish torpedo bombers it could put into the air, and Tovey now ordered them all up to go after the *Bismarck*. It was his hope that they might be able

A British officer demonstrates how a torpedo is attached to a Swordfish bomber.

to do enough damage to the German ship so that it would be slowed down and his ships would be able to catch up to it.

The commanders of the whole British Navy also had to ponder what to do. Like Tovey, they still feared that the *Bismarck* was going to make a run for the Atlantic, and they knew Tovey's force might not be able to catch it before it did. They simply *had* to put enough ships between the Atlantic and the places where the *Bismarck* might try to get into it, to stop the German ship. So what they did was to order every single British warship in the Atlantic to drop whatever it was doing and go hunting for the *Bismarck*. This meant that every British convoy in the Atlantic would be completely without protection—a very dangerous gamble. But a total of fifty-six surface ships and eight submarines were now moving from all directions, seeking the German battleship.

Admiral Lütjens had no idea of the enormous force that was now trying to catch his ship. The *Bismarck* was proceeding toward St. Nazaire with the three British warships—the *Prince of Wales*, the *Suffolk*, and the *Norfolk*—still keeping pace at a discreet distance.

But at eleven-thirty that night, the *Bismarck* suddenly came under unexpected attack. The Swordfish torpedo bombers that Admiral Tovey had sent out had finally reached their goal. They had been flying for some time, and at one point had nearly launched an attack on an American Coast Guard ship that their squadron leader momentarily mistook for the *Bismarck*. Now, through a gap in the clouds, they sighted the German ship and began to move in. Even though it was nearly midnight, there was still enough light in the arctic sky for them to see what they had to do.

A torpedo bomber was an airplane designed to launch a torpedo at a ship. It did this simply by flying just above the surface of the water, straight at the ship, getting as close as possible, and dropping the torpedo, which was fastened to its underside. When the torpedo hit the water, a small motor in its rear drove it swiftly along the surface in a straight line. If the pilot of the aircraft had gotten close enough and dropped the torpedo at the right moment, it might strike the ship and explode, causing serious damage. If it missed, it would just keep on going until its motor ran down.

Warships had devised a number of ways of dealing with such attacks. The ship would steer in sharp zigzags, making it difficult for a pilot to drop his torpedo with any accuracy. Meanwhile, the ship's antiaircraft guns poured streams of machine-gun bullets and explosive shells into the air at the plane. Another technique was to fire into the water directly ahead of an oncoming plane, causing a cluster of huge water-spouts to erupt upward. A plane running into a waterspout would be knocked cartwheeling into the sea.

At the sight of the planes, the *Bismarck* increased speed and began to zigzag. The ship's twenty-eight antiaircraft guns opened up, turning it into a fire-spitting monster. The planes attacked from several different directions, some flying no more than 6 or 7 feet above the water as they made their torpedo-launching approaches. The sea around the *Bismarck* came alive with waterspouts caused by the ship's guns.

Suddenly, the chatter of the *Bismarck*'s antiaircraft guns was momentarily drowned out by a sharp explosion, and the ship gave a shudder. A torpedo had hit!

The groups of seamen and officers responsible for damage control and fire fighting rushed to the area of the hit. They found that the torpedo had struck the heaviest part of the armor on the hull, but the armor had done its job and there was no damage. However, a number of men who had been close to the explosion had been violently hurled in all directions by the concussion. Six had suffered broken bones and one had been killed—the *Bismarck*'s first casualty.

Having dropped all their torpedoes, the Swordfish bombers turned away and roared off to find their carrier before darkness fell. They all made it back safely. The flyers had done their best, bravely risking their lives, but the attack had been a failure. They would have to report that the *Bismarck* was still on course, moving at a good speed.

But actually, the *Bismarck* was having some problems. The high speed and sharp zigzagging during the air attack had caused the temporary repairs to the shellholes in the hull, made in the battle against the *Hood* and the *Prince of Wales*, to come apart, and the ship was taking in water again. New repairs were quickly made, but the ship's speed was now down to 31 miles an hour.

In the Denmark Strait in late May, darkness falls at about two o'clock in the morning. Admiral Lütjens was awaiting the coming of darkness, because under its cover he intended to try to break free of the three British ships that had been shadowing the *Bismarck* since the previous morning. Lütjens had noticed that all three ships were staying on the *Bismarck*'s port side (the left side of a ship when facing the ship's front.) When night came, if the other side, the starboard side, was still left unguarded, Lütjens hoped to steal away in that direction.

Darkness finally settled over the icy waters. Lütjens kept the *Bismarck* on its course while the ship's radarmen checked and rechecked to see if they could pick up any signal showing ships to starboard. Nothing.

Shortly after three o'clock, the *Bismarck* increased its speed and turned to starboard. It steered in almost a full circle, then finally turned southeast, the direction of St. Nazaire. It moved steadily through the darkness.

The *Bismarck* was not visible to the British ships during the short arctic night, but the *Suffolk* was always able to keep track of the German ship by means of its excellent radar system. However, the *Suffolk* and its two companions were steering slow zigzag courses for fear of German submarines, and each time the *Suffolk* "zigged" away from the direction of the *Bismarck*, it lost radar contact for about twenty minutes until it "zagged" back. Therefore, when it lost contact at 3:06, its radarmen were unworried; they expected to pick up the German ship again by three-thirty.

But at three-thirty the screen was blank. With growing concern, the radarmen watched the shaft of light on the screen make sweep after sweep without picking up the telltale shape that indicated the presence of a ship. At five o'clock, a regretful message was sent to British naval headquarters. "Have lost contact with the enemy." The *Bismarck* had broken free.

Chapter 6

A FRANTIC SEARCH, A LUCKY FIND

There was dismay throughout British naval headquarters on the morning of May 25 when it was learned that the *Bismarck* had escaped and was roaming free. Admiral Tovey's Home Fleet ships had actually drawn to within 100 miles of the German battleship, with a good chance of eventually catching up to it, and now it had vanished. The navy's commanders were once more faced with the horrifying possibility that the *Bismarck* would be able to get into the Atlantic, where there were now unprotected merchant convoys that it could utterly destroy. Prime Minister Churchill, badly worried, told the commanders, "You must sink the *Bismarck*!"

A frantic search began. To make things even more difficult, the weather turned bad, the sea grew rough, visibility became poor. The hours moved relentlessly on, turning early morning into midmorning, and still the *Bismarck* had not been found.

But aboard the *Bismarck* neither Admiral Lütjens nor anyone else was even aware that the ship had actually escaped from the three British vessels that had hung onto it for thirty-one hours. They could not be seen, but everyone assumed that was because of the poor visibility. However, at 8:46 that morning, the *Bismarck* received a radio message from German naval headquarters advising Admiral Lütjens that messages being picked up from the *Suffolk* seemed to indicate that the British no longer knew where the *Bismarck* was. "Have impression that contact has been broken," naval headquarters stated.

Lütjens apparently did not believe this. For some reason he continued to think that the *Suffolk* and its two companions were somewhere nearby, still keeping track of the *Bismarck* by radar. Thus, in his mind there was no reason for the *Bismarck* to try to be secretive, such as keeping radio silence (not sending any messages) so that the British couldn't get a "fix" on the *Bismarck*'s position. This caused him to make a serious mistake. At nine o'clock in the morning he sent a long radio message to German naval headquarters. If he had not sent that message, the British would have had no way of finding where the *Bismarck* was except by hunting for it. But now, the message was picked up by radio stations in Britain, which could locate where it was coming from and thus determine the *Bismarck*'s position. By about ten-thirty, British naval headquarters sent Admiral Tovey a message providing an estimation of where the German ship could be found.

However, what could have been a bit of very bad luck for the *Bismarck* actually worked in its favor. When Tovey had the information from naval headquarters refigured aboard his ship, it seemed to indicate several different possible positions for the *Bismarck*. Tovey had to choose one, and the one that made the most sense in his mind seemed to indicate that the *Bismarck* was heading north toward the waters off Norway. Accordingly, Tovey turned his ships northward and began heading *away* from the *Bismarck*'s actual position.

But the commanders at naval headquarters had doubts about this choice. They made new computations based on the *Bismarck*'s known position some hours earlier, and were able to determine that the ship seemed to be heading toward the west coast of France, as indeed it was. After some consideration, Admiral Tovey agreed they were right. By six o'clock that night, he had turned his force southeast, on a course that should cross the *Bismarck*'s path.

But long before that happened, Admiral Lütjens had finally become convinced that his ship had indeed broken free, and ordered radio silence. The word that the *Bismarck* was running free spread to the crew and morale soared. The German sailors rejoiced over their ship's success. They had sunk the great *Hood*, had crippled the *Prince of Wales,* and now they had a good chance of getting to safety. But then Admiral Lütjens made a short speech that sobered them. While he praised their victory over the *Hood,* he pointed out that the British were surely gathering their forces to bring them all into action against the *Bismarck,* and there was still a good possibility that the *Bismarck* would be caught before it reached St. Nazaire, and might have to fight against overwhelming odds. "For us seamen," he told them, "the choice is now victory or death!"

The speech made the crew's morale sink a bit. But then someone came up with an idea that might help the *Bismarck* to reach port without having to fight. The idea was to *disguise* the ship by giving it an additional smokestack. The second smokestack would be a fake, built out of canvas, wood, and wire. With two smokestacks the *Bismarck* would actually resemble a *British* ship from a distance or from the air, so it might be ignored by any British ships or planes that were looking for the German ship with its single smokestack. Work began on building the fake smokestack, and when it was finished it was painted gray to match the rest of the ship.

The day of May 25 came to an end with the *Bismarck* still free and undiscovered by the British ships seeking it. With every hour that passed, the ship drew closer to safety at St. Nazaire. German naval headquarters sent word to Admiral Lütjens that planes of the German Air Force were ready to provide protection for the *Bismarck* as soon as it was close enough to the French coast, and three German destroyers were coming out to help it make its way safely into the port. At four-thirty on the morning of May 26, Lütjens made an announcement to the crew, telling them that by noon the *Bismarck* would be in range of German planes and ships and would be safe. Morale soared again.

At the time Lütjens made this announcement, the *Bismarck* was about three quarters of the way past Ireland. An hour and a half earlier, two airplanes known as Catalina flying boats had taken off from northern Ireland to make a long-range search for the *Bismarck* in the waters off the Irish coast.

A Catalina was an American-built airplane. It was a big, bulky aircraft that truly was a flying boat, because it could "land" in, float on, and take off from water. A Catalina could fly almost 2,000 miles away from its base before having to turn around and go back, so these were excellent planes for making long-range searches over the ocean. The United States had given the British Royal Air Force a number of Catalinas, and had also provided seventeen American pilots to help the British learn full use of the planes. (This was done in strict secrecy, because the United States was not at war with Germany at this time, and for American servicemen to be helping the British against Germany was a violation of international law.)

One of the Catalinas flying over the ocean on the morning of May 26 was piloted by an Englishman, but the copilot was an American, Ensign Leonard Smith of the United States Navy. Visibility was poor, but at about 10:15, Smith caught sight of a ship through a hole in the clouds. The Catalina circled around for another look.

For some reason, now unknown, the crew of the *Bismarck* had not yet put up the fake smokestack, which was simply lying on the deck. So when the ship was sighted again, there was no doubt in the minds of the two men on the Catalina as to what

Contact with the Bismarck *was re-established on May 26, when the crew of a Catalina flying boat spotted the battleship.*

ship they were looking at. They were even more sure it was the enemy ship when it suddenly erupted with a cascade of antiaircraft fire that filled the air around them with black bursts of smoke and made the Catalina rock from the concussions. Moving off to a safer distance, they immediately reported their find by radio, giving all the necessary information— "One battleship bearing 240 degrees, five miles, course 150 degrees. My position 49.33 north, 21.47 west."

The *Bismarck*, which had been loose for thirty-one hours, had been caught again.

Chapter 7

THE TRIUMPH OF THE TORPEDO BOMBERS

Even though the British naval commanders now knew exactly where to find the *Bismarck*, their situation was far from good. Admiral Tovey's force—the battleship *King George V*, with five cruisers and five destroyers—was 135 miles north of the German ship, which was a long way to go. Furthermore, Tovey's ships had burned a lot of fuel by making their long, useless jaunt north and back, and were now running very low. Two of the ships Tovey had started out with, the battleship *Repulse* and the aircraft carrier *Victorious*, had already been forced to turn back to the nearest base to refuel. The battleship *Prince of Wales*, which had been shadowing the *Bismarck* with the cruisers *Norfolk* and *Suffolk*, had also had to drop out of the chase. It did not look as if any British battleships were going to be able to engage the *Bismarck* in combat before it reached the waters off the French coast that were protected by German submarines and airplanes. And by themselves, the smaller ships, cruisers, and destroyers would not, of course, be any match for the big German battleship.

The only hope was to somehow cripple the *Bismarck* so that

it would be slowed down enough for a battleship and some smaller ships to catch up to it and fight it. At the moment, the only chance of crippling the German ship was with aircraft. This meant that everything was in the hands of Admiral Somerville's group, known as Force H, which had come up from the Mediterranean Sea—the battle cruiser *Renown*, the cruiser *Sheffield*, and the aircraft carrier *Ark Royal*, from which Swordfish torpedo bombers could take off to attack the *Bismarck* from the sky.

The ships of Force H were now the closest British ships to the *Bismarck*, about 100 miles away, which was close enough for the Swordfish. At 1:15 on the afternoon of the twenty-sixth, three hours after the *Bismarck* had been found, the cruiser *Sheffield* was sent forward to locate it exactly and pinpoint it for the torpedo bombers. At 2:50, fourteen Swordfish with their torpedoes slung underneath rose up from the *Ark Royal* and headed for the position radioed in by the *Sheffield*. One hour later they arrived and immediately roared in to attack.

The attack was a near disaster. The sea was high with choppy waves from a storm, and visibility was very poor. The Swordfish bombers saw a tossing ship and attacked it, each plane rushing in to launch its torpedo. Only moments later did the pilot in command realize to his horror that the ship was the *Sheffield*, not the *Bismarck*! The torpedo bombers were attacking one of their own ships! The *Sheffield* dodged and turned to avoid the torpedoes racing through the water toward it. Fortunately for the British, every one of the torpedoes either missed or exploded before striking the ship.

As well as nearly being a tragedy, the misdirected attack was a bad waste of precious time. The *Bismarck* was still on course and now hours closer to reaching safety. Admiral Tovey, notified by a radio message from Admiral Somerville that the attack had not accomplished anything, was bitterly disappointed. He sent a message back to Somerville to let him know that if something couldn't be done to slow the *Bismarck* by midnight, Tovey would have to stop pursuing the German ships in order to let his ships refuel. This would mean that all the tremendous effort the British Navy had made to catch the *Bismarck* and sink it would have been wasted.

Somerville tried again. At 7:10, fifteen more Swordfish torpedo bombers took off from the *Ark Royal* and headed toward the *Bismarck*'s position. The sea was still stormy and daylight was fading. Everyone from Admiral Somerville to the pilots of the torpedo bombers knew that this would be the last attack, the last possible chance to keep the *Bismarck* from getting away.

The planes passed over the *Sheffield,* which was still shadowing the *Bismarck,* at eight o'clock. It signaled the *Bismarck*'s position to them and they turned in that direction. But upon reaching the place where the *Bismarck* was supposed to be, they found nothing. Turning back, they flew over the *Sheffield* again. It gave them a new direction and once more they headed off. At about eight-thirty they finally sighted the *Bismarck.*

On the ship an aircraft alarm was sounded and the antiaircraft guns were manned. The planes roared overhead at a high altitude, making a final check to be sure they had the right target. For a time they vanished from the *Bismarck*'s sight. Then, suddenly, they were back, coming out of low clouds in a scattered formation, heading straight for the battleship. The air was shattered by the blasts and clatter of the antiaircraft guns, the sounds of which could be heard on the *Sheffield,* miles away. The *Bismarck* began to zigzag sharply.

Two of the Swordfish bombers came roaring at the ship almost side by side. Just as the *Bismarck* began to turn in one of its zigzags, they dropped their torpedoes simultaneously. The long cigarlike shapes raced through the water like deadly sharks in search of prey. Suddenly, there were two explosions, one after another, and the *Bismarck* gave a violent lurch.

Everyone on the battleship knew it had been hit, but they

all continued their duties whatever those might be. The planes were now heading off, but the cruiser *Sheffield* had come into view some distance away. The *Bismarck*'s gunnery officer snapped out orders and the 15-inch guns thundered two salvos. On the *Sheffield* the air was suddenly filled with whirring bits of metal as shells exploded in the water close to the ship. Twelve men went down with bloody wounds. The *Sheffield* made a quick turn and retreated, belching out a smoke screen to hide its movement.

The *Bismarck*'s damage control teams went to work to see what the torpedo hits had done to the ship. One of the torpedoes had struck the hull near the middle of the ship, but the armor had once again done its job and there was no damage. But the result of the other torpedo's hit was another story. It had exploded near the rear of the ship and torn a gaping hole in the hull. Water was pouring into the compartment where the ship's steering was done, and the rudder, which controlled the ship's direction, was jammed. The jam had taken place while the *Bismarck* was making a zigzag turn, and the ship was now turned *away* from the direction of St. Nazaire and was headed in a direction that would take it straight into the ships of Admiral Tovey's Home Fleet!

This was exactly what the British had been praying for, and more. Not only had the *Bismarck* been stopped from reaching the coast of France, but the British ships would not even have to chase it down—it was coming right to them! Admiral Lütjens knew this was almost certainly the end. At 9:40 he sent a message to German naval headquarters. "Ship unable to maneuver. We will fight to the last round." (By this, he meant the *Bismarck* would fight until its last shell was fired.)

The *Bismarck*'s captain, Lindemann, tried everything possible to free the rudder, with sudden changes in speed and quick changeovers from one engine to another. Nothing worked. Men in diving gear tried to force their way into the flooded

Swordfish torpedo bombers from the aircraft carrier Ark Royal *did significant damage to the* Bismarck. *One of their torpedoes jammed the* Bismarck's *rudder.*

steering compartment to reach the rudder mechanism, but one after another failed. Finally, a man did manage to get to the mechanism, but it was so badly jammed he could not budge it. By midnight all attempts to free the rudder were given up. The *Bismarck* continued to head straight toward Tovey's oncoming ships.

Even while all the attempts to fix the rudder were being made, the crewmen of the *Bismarck* continued to carry out their regular duties. The ship was still on full alert and most men were at their battle stations. At eleven o'clock, British destroyers were sighted, and the *Bismarck*'s guns began to thunder again.

There were five destroyers, although the men on the *Bismarck* could not tell this in the stormy darkness. The destroyers that had been assigned to Admiral Tovey's force were rushing up from the south to join him, and their course had led them right into the *Bismarck*. They had never fought a battleship and they weren't really designed to fight battleships, but this seemed too good an opportunity to let slip away. They attempted to move in close, very quickly, and launch torpedoes. But the wind was blowing furiously and high waves were sweeping across the decks of all the ships. The destroyers had a very difficult time maneuvering, and the *Bismarck* had a hard time pointing its guns, which caused its shells to fall into the sea. The most horrifying part of the battle for the destroyers' radarmen was that they could actually see the *Bismarck*'s shells coming straight at them as swiftly moving blips on the radar screen. Tensely, they would wait until the blips suddenly vanished, indicating that the shells had hit the water, when they would let out sighs of relief. Throughout the night the destroyers kept up their attack and the *Bismarck*'s guns continued to roar at them, yet not one torpedo struck the German battleship and not one of the *Bismarck*'s shells hit a British ship.

All this time, Admiral Lütjens had been sending messages to the German naval headquarters, reporting the events. At a few minutes before two o'clock, Adolf Hitler, the leader of the German nation, sent a message to Lütjens that said: "I thank you in the name of the German people." Moments later a message came that was addressed to the *Bismarck*'s entire crew. "All Germany is with you. What can be done, will be done. Your performance of duty will strengthen our people in the struggle for its destiny." This was basically just a farewell speech, and it showed that Hitler believed the *Bismarck* was doomed.

The dawn of May 27 crept into the sky a little before six o'clock. The destroyers now pulled back out of sight, disappearing into the misty curtains of rain. They had not done any damage to the *Bismarck*, but they had kept track of its position for Admiral Tovey. Every sailor on the German battleship knew that at any moment British battleships and cruisers would come into sight, and the *Bismarck*'s last battle would begin.

Chapter 8

THE DEATH OF THE *BISMARCK*

The mood aboard the *Bismarck* on the morning of May 27 was, of course, somber. For nearly two days the crewmen had felt sure they would reach St. Nazaire and safety, but now they knew there was no hope. In the coming battle many of them, perhaps all of them, would die.

The mood aboard the British battleship *King George V* was, naturally, very different. During the past ten hours it had gone from bitter disappointment, to puzzlement, to elation. At ten-thirty the night before, Admiral Tovey had received a message from the *Ark Royal* informing him that all the Swordfish torpedo bombers had returned from the second attack on the *Bismarck* and the pilots had reported only one hit, on the middle of the ship. Tovey was desolate. A hit amidships wouldn't do the kind of damage he had hoped for. It seemed sure that his last chance of catching the *Bismarck* had vanished.

Then he began getting puzzling messages, one from a scout plane, followed by one from the cruiser *Sheffield*, still keeping an eye on the *Bismarck*. Both messages stated that the *Bismarck* had turned north and was sailing straight for him! After a time he began getting similar reports from the destroyers that had attacked the German ship. It was obvious to them that something was wrong with the *Bismarck*'s steering. It appeared as if it could only head north. So, by the dawn of the twenty-seventh, Admiral Tovey was jubilant. The *Bismarck* could not escape him any longer. Besides his force, a number of other British ships were now converging on the stricken German battleship. The cruiser *Norfolk* was coming fast from the north. Another cruiser, the *Dorsetshire*, was coming from the west. And Admiral Somerville's Force H was hurrying up from the southwest.

The first to arrive was the *Norfolk*. It sighted the *Bismarck* at a distance of 9 miles at a little before eight o'clock. It pulled back out of gun range and sent a message to Admiral Tovey giving the *Bismarck*'s exact position. Some time later, Tovey's ship, *King George V*, and the battleship *Rodney* were seen by watchers on the *Bismarck* coming over the horizon.

With the appearance of the *Norfolk* the alarm had gone off on the *Bismarck*, and all hands were at their battle stations. The fourth gunnery officer, peering into his telescopic sighting device, saw the two British battleships heading straight toward him. The *Bismarck*'s eight big guns were going to be outnumbered by the enemy battleships' nineteen!

The British battleships had come to do what they were designed for—*pound* an enemy! *King George V* mounted ten 14-inch guns and sixteen 5 1/4-inch guns, and had as much as 15 inches of armor on part of its hull and up to 13 inches on its main gun turrets. It was 745 feet long, with a crew of about 1,644 men. The *Rodney* had nine 16-inch guns—as big as they came—and twelve 6-inch ones. Its hull armor was 14 inches thick, the armor on its main gun turrets went up to 16 inches. It was 710 feet long, and its crew was 1,314 strong.

The *Rodney* fired first, at a range of 12 1/2 miles, its big guns shattering the air with their explosions. It took a full minute for those huge heavy shells to go arching across that distance, then

The Norfolk *fires a salvo at the* Bismarck.

they crashed into the water, sending up a cluster of 75-foot high splashes some distance from the *Bismarck*. At almost the same instant, the *King George V*'s guns erupted. The shells from these also plunged into the water.

The time was now 8:49. The *Bismarck*'s forward guns spouted flame and smoke, launching four shells at the *Rodney*. All were near misses. The *Norfolk*, which had crept into range, now fired its eight 4-inch guns. A few minutes later, the *Dorsetshire*'s guns opened up from a range of 11 1/4 miles. The *Bismarck* was under fire from all directions, and shells were beginning to hit. Its guns continued to concentrate on the two British battleships, but it was starting to take heavy punishment.

The *King George V* and the *Rodney* moved steadily forward,

The Rodney *fires her 16-inch guns.*

making their gun range shorter and shorter. Their shells were slamming into the *Bismarck*, which could not maneuver to avoid this fire because of its damaged rudder. At about 9:02 a shell from the *Rodney* exploded on the *Bismarck*'s front gun turret, leaving two guns bent downward and unable to fire. The *Bismarck* was down to six main guns against nineteen. With those six it kept firing. Then there was a hit on the second forward turret, and its guns were left pointing high into the air to one side, out of action. Now the *Bismarck* had only four main guns left.

A shell crashed into the *Bismarck*'s main fire-control (gun aiming) station, demolishing it. Control of the four remaining guns went to the secondary fire-control unit. Then that, too, was knocked out of action, and the guns had to begin firing on their own, the gunners picking out their targets by sight. By now the *Bismarck* was badly hurt. Fires were glowing here and there on its lower decks, smoke billowed up out of openings, bent and crushed hatch covers (metal doors) littered the main deck, dead and wounded men lay everywhere.

The *King George V* and the *Rodney* continued to move relentlessly forward. The range for their guns dropped to 4 miles, then 3, then 2. This was point-blank range, at which almost every shell fired was a hit. The *Bismarck* was being pounded to death, and it was a shambles. Much of the superstructure—the parts of the ship above the main deck—had been turned into twisted piles of scrap metal. The bridge was demolished, the last two gun turrets mangled beyond use. The fires on the lower decks had spread, and a volcano-like eruption of black smoke was now pouring up from the ship.

Finally the command came: "Clear ship for scuttling." This meant that the *Bismarck* was no longer able to fight; the crew was being ordered to leave it. The sea cocks, valves in the ship's hull, were to be opened to allow water to flood into the ship and help it sink so that it couldn't be captured. The battle was over and the fatally wounded *Bismarck* was going to die.

The men on the British warships could see that the *Bismarck* was finished, even though it had not yet sunk. The big guns of the *King George V* and the *Rodney* fell silent. It was now 10:15, and Admiral Tovey, worried about the extremely low fuel situation of both ships, ordered them to turn away and make for home. The cruiser *Dorsetshire* moved forward to finish off the *Bismarck*. At 10:20 it launched two torpedoes into the battleship's starboard side, then steered around and put a third torpedo into the port side at 10:36.

The *Bismarck* was finally sinking. Its rear end was deep in the water, the front end was rearing upward toward the sky, and the whole ship was leaning over to the port side. All the lifeboats

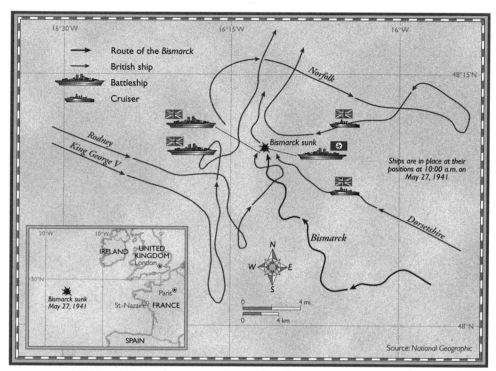

Sinking the Bismarck

had been smashed by the explosions of British shells that had hit near them. The *Bismarck* crewmen still alive knew they had to go into the icy water, which was covered with patches of flaming oil that had leaked out of the ship, and float there for as long as it might take to be rescued—if they were ever found! They all had on inflated life jackets, and they jumped overboard singly and in groups, swimming hard to get far enough away from the ship so that when it went under, the suction created wouldn't pull them down with it. Keeping 150 yards or more away, they floated, bobbing up and down like corks, and watched their ship sink.

It has always been the tradition in most navies that when a ship sinks, its captain goes down with it. The *Bismarck*'s sailors, wallowing in the water, looked back to see Captain Lindemann

Bismarck *survivors cling to lifelines thrown to them from a British ship.*

standing on the ship's side, with his hand raised to his cap in salute. Very slowly, the *Bismarck* and *Kapitän zur See* Ernst Lindemann went down together. The ship rolled over with its underside facing upward and bubbles rising around it. Then it sank.

None of the ship's survivors had any knowledge of what had become of Admiral Lütjens. It was presumed that he was still on the *Bismarck*, dead or badly wounded, when it went down. Altogether, more than 1,900 German sailors perished as a result of the battle and the sinking of the ship. A total of 110 survivors were eventually picked up by British ships and another 3 were picked up by a German submarine that later came to the site of the battle.

The *Bismarck* sank at 10:39 on the morning of May 27, 1941. Its destruction was the end of Germany's efforts to destroy British shipping with surface warships. Five days after the *Bismarck* sank, the *Prinz Eugen* slipped into the port of Brest, on the French coast, where the German battleships *Scharnhorst* and *Gneisenau* were huddled for safety. No German battleship or cruiser ever again tried to make for the Atlantic.

Epilogue

During those days in May 1941, much of the world was intently watching the contest between the *Bismarck* and the British Navy. In America, daily news reports on the radio described events as they were happening. Most Americans were sharply opposed to the beliefs and methods of the Nazi government in Germany, and favored helping Britain, so there was a general hope that the British would be able to catch the German ship and prevent it from doing any harm. In Canada, Australia, New Zealand, and other countries that were part of what was then known as the British Empire, there was of course widespread desire that the British forces would sink the *Bismarck*. People were gripped by excitement as the drama of the sea chase and the final one-sided battle drew to a close.

As far as its effect on the war was concerned, the struggle between the *Bismarck* and the British Navy really didn't amount to much. The *Bismarck* was not able to accomplish what it was sent out to do—neither it nor the *Prinz Eugen* ever got to the Atlantic, and British shipping was not hurt by them. Nor, despite all the claims of the *Bismarck* as the world's most power-

A crowd gathered in front of a bulletin board in New York City's Times Square learns the fate of the Bismarck.

ful warship, did it really cause much damage to the British Navy. The destruction of the *Hood*, while a serious blow to British pride and a terrible loss to the families of its crew, did not affect the navy's overall power—the damage to the *Prince of Wales* was only slight, and the *Bismarck*'s guns didn't even hit any other ships. The loss of the *Bismarck* was far more serious to Germany's hopes and plans. The *Bismarck* had the shortest career and took the worst pounding of any battleship in history.

* * *

Interest in the *Bismarck's* story continued in the years following the war, with new books about the *Bismarck* appearing in every decade for a time. A motion picture called *Sink the Bismarck!* was made in Hollywood in 1960. Models of the *Bismarck* abounded in hobby shops.

In 1988 a group of scientists and businessmen headed by Dr. Robert Ballard (who located the sunken *Titanic*) formed an expedition to search for the sunken *Bismarck*, using a small submersible craft carrying television and photographic equipment that could be operated by remote control. Lowered from a ship by a thick cable, the submersible was dragged back and forth over areas where the *Bismarck* was thought to be.

On June 8, 1989, forty-eight years and twelve days after it sank, the *Bismarck* was found just about 3 miles down on the floor of the Atlantic, some 600 miles off the coast of France. It is lying right side up, with the huge painted Nazi swastika emblem, which has come to be a symbol of evil, still clearly visible on the front portion of the deck. The ship is in surprisingly good condition, although all of its main gun turrets and parts of its superstructure are gone.

The story of the struggle between the whole British Navy and the *Bismarck* is one of the great sea stories of all time. It will probably continue to be a story that interests and excites people for many years to come. Some day, the *Bismarck* may be raised out of the ocean and put on display somewhere, as a historic relic of World War II.

Index

Page numbers in *italics* refer to illustrations.